The Black Book of Forex Trading

A Proven Method to Become a Profitable Trader in Four Months and Reach Your Financial Freedom by Doing It

Paul Langer

No part of this publication may be reproduced, distributed, or transmitted in any form by any means, including photocopying, recording, or other electronic or mechanical methods, or by any information storage and retrieval system without the prior written permission of the publisher, except in the case of very brief quotations embodied in critical reviews and certain other noncommercial uses permitted by copyright law.
Copyright © Alura Publishing 2015

All rights reserved.

ISBN-13: **978-1517760571**

DEDICATION

This book is dedicated to all the struggling traders trying to reach their dream of financial freed

CONTENTS

DEDICATION iii

CONTENTS v

Disclaimer i

INTRODUCTION 1

How to lose $50,000 working very hard (Only to earn them back many times over) 7

A strange meeting, a strange man, and some wine 10

THE INFAMOUS "A-HA" MOMENT 14

The Right Mental Framing (or, why traders don't make money) 16

TO DEMO OR NOT TO DEMO 22

WHY TRADE THE FOREX MARKETS 24

BASICS OF TRADING 27

Trends and ranges 27

Support and Resistance 29

Let's talk about strategies 31

Position trading Strategy "Big Bulls and Bears" 32

A Swing Trading Strategy 39

A Scalping Strategy 45

The Unexpected "Holy Grail" of trading, or how to calculate your position size ... 52

The Black Swans 57

The Importance of Having a Trading Plan 60

Your 6-step blueprint to become a profitable trader. 68

Final thoughts 70

DISCLAIMER

This publication is designed to provide accurate and authoritative information in regard to the subject matter covered. It is sold with the understanding that the publisher is not engaged in rendering legal, accounting, investing or other professional services. If legal advice or other professional assistance is required, the services of a competent professional person should be sought.

No responsibility or liability is assumed by the publisher for any injury, damage or financial or personal loss sustained to persons or property from the use of this information, personal or otherwise, either directly or indirectly.

While every effort has been made to ensure reliability and accuracy of the information within, all liability, negligence or otherwise, from any use, misuse or abuse of the operation of any methods, strategies, instructions or ideas contained in the material herein, is the sole responsibility of the reader.

Any copyrights not held by Publisher are owned by their respective authors.

All information is generalized, presented for informational purposes only and presented "as is" without warranty or guarantee of any kind. Neither the Publisher or the author shall be liable to you or anyone else for any inaccuracy, error or omission, regardless of cause, in the work or for any damages resulting therefrom. The publisher has no responsibility for the content of any information accessed through the work. Under no circumstances shall the Publisher be liable for any indirect, incidental, special, punitive, consequential or similar damages that result from the use of or inability to use the work, even if any of them has ben advised of the possibility of such damages. This limitation liability shall apply to any claim or cause whatsoever whether such claim or cause arises in contract, or otherwise.

All trademarks and brands referred to in this book are for illustrative purposes only, are the property of their respective owners and not affiliate with this publication in any way.

INTRODUCTION

I've always loved the idea of being independent. From the time I was 10 years old, I was looking for ways to save some money from the small amount of change my parents gave me, or to do some tiny business, like selling candy to my schoolmates so I could get a few pennies for me. I knew if I had a little money saved I could just buy that comic book I wanted by myself, or that other video game I liked or some new strings for my guitar, and my parents wouldn't be able to tell me "no." Not that they would tell me "no" very often, but the choice was mine if I had the money myself, and that was enough to motivate me to find ways to make extra money here and there.

After all this years – I am 37 now – I didn't change much. I was never very good at keeping jobs and mostly I have been starting businesses and doing freelance jobs since I was 20. But, despite my personal feelings about money, I believe that, in the times we're living, the ultimate goal is to have financial freedom, maybe even more than any other kind of freedom. I believe we have, as a generation, already discovered that the world is too big to be trapped within one job, one career, one country, let alone one city. If we control our own supply of money, we're free, we own our time, and we can decide what to do with it.

Most of my friends, and people I know around the world, are dreaming about going for some time to live to Asia, to South America, to Africa, to Europe, Mexico, USA, Australia, or to any place far away from where they currently reside.

It doesn't matter if you are married and have children, in that case you may want to take your family with you, so the kids can learn another culture and another language; or, if you are single, you want to go and live some grand adventures so you can feel you are living your life to the fullest.

Entrepreneurship is growing and many people are trying their luck at selling something, starting some business on the side, doing some freelance job or at least dreaming of it and preparing themselves to find the right moment to start doing it.

For our parents and grandparents generation, these dreams of traveling far and finding adventure somewhere else on the globe, or starting a business on their own, running from the idea of the financial stability a real job will give you, was more or less an illusion. Most people were trapped, or self-trapped, in the idea of having a job, a family, a house, and living a little better each year and saving for retirement.

Maybe because of the housing crisis, the Internet era, social networks, the higher rates of unemployment all around the world, or everything that is happening together, we've learned that the old values of the "perfect" life are no longer valid. This has opened to us the doors and our eyes to find our future somehow in a different manner.

We've seen 22-year-old guys selling their companies (some of them without even make a dime of profit) for billions, and we've all read stories about Internet entrepreneurs, traders, marketers and all kind of people who are living the "great life" but began in a very similar ground of where you and I could be standing now.

The good news is that you don't need to be the next Mark Zuckerberg to live an independent life. You don't need a degree from an Ivy League school so you may enter in into this "elite" group of people, because there's no gatekeeper here. And, yes, I know, because I've done it myself. Trading and the Forex market is a way of gaining this …the highly regarded financial freedom.

IMPORTANT WORD OF ADVICE:

It's very necessary for me to tell you, before you read any further and maybe waste your valuable time. This is not an advanced or comprehensive book covered with a lot of complicated strategies. This book doesn't rely on highly sophisticated math, complex indicators, and academic analysis of the markets or any of the sorts. If you are an advanced trader and are looking for the new high tech sophistication on finding your entry, you won't find it here.

In the beginning of my trading career I was also trying to trade with difficult to understand and highly sophisticated systems based on complexity and they just didn't work for me. I'll not say they will not work for you or the next guy, everyone is different and have different needs, but I've found out that to be profitable in my trading, simplicity was a powerful and invaluable tool.

Why am I saying this to you? I've found some people that have been disappointed and even angry to find out that this book doesn't have super advanced complicated extensive trading techniques and, if you are looking for that, please stop reading and just give back the book and we can part as friends.

In this book you will find my PERSONAL story on how I became a profitable trader in the Forex Markets, it's not a comprehensive text book about trading covering a great deal of strategies or an extensive description of all about Forex trading. I don't pretend that this will be the only book you'll read in your life to understand everything there is to understand about trading.

Yes it also has a few short chapters about my personal story, I thought they would be interesting to read for many of you, since they'll show you I am a human being and I have had quite a hard time becoming a profitable trader and, in the meantime, I lost my life savings and then found a way to earn them back from my trading.

If you are not interested in my personal story just skip the chapters and move on to the more technical ones. They are all well labeled in the Table of Contents.

Many of us have spent thousands of dollars learning to trade, courses, mentors, signals, robots, etc. So please take into consideration the power of a simple affordable short book like this one. I am sure it will help you in your trading but please understand it's just a book, not a mentor or a full trading course.

My main purpose on writing this book is to show you how you too can become profitable trading, basically by adjusting a few of your current habits and if you grasp some concepts that maybe you were not aware of, even if you don't spend the next ten years learning all the technical and fundamental strategies known to man, or if you are working a full time job or simply don't have the personality to stare at the screen all your day but still, want to make trading a viable option for earning extra income or even make a living out of it.

I'll do show you a few strategies that work for me, but they are not the core concept I want to communicate from this book. In my opinion there's way more important subjects and concepts to grasp than to know a thousand techniques on how to find an entry or use indicators to find entries, and I will speak about these concepts through the book.

I am a profitable trader and I have been making consistent money from the markets for many years now and, if you read books from real traders, you will find that most of the times they use surprisingly simple strategies to find their entries.

I've also learn that to overcomplicate yourself doesn't normally work in the trading business, because you will ad some extra variables on top of everything you already are trying to cop with when you are trading.

Is trading a viable option for everyone? Is it for you? Can anyone trade profitably?

I can tell you it's not for everyone. You need habits and discipline; if you start improvising and following your guts, most likely you will fail (I am this person who loves improvising, I play jazz and all my life have gone using my gut feeling for everything, so I had a hard time learning how to do it, but in the end it is quite easy, and you can devote your creativity somewhere else, because you will have the time).

If you can't stick to a plan and follow your own rules, if you get impatient and change your strategy every time you lose a trade, or if you can't deal with losing money, because trading is about winning and losing, too (but being profitable at the end of the month/year), most likely you will fail, too.

But, if you can just focus on repeating a series of simple analysis tasks; if you want to use trading as a platform for doing other things in life that you love; if you don't want to be a slave to the screen, like you are in your regular office job; and have a life of your own, then you will have a chance to succeed.

I wrote this book with the idea of helping traders who, like I was a few years ago, are struggling to make money consistently, or are constantly losing money. In the book you will find all the elements necessary to make the shift and become a successful trader, although if you are a complete newbie and have no idea about pips, pairs, brokers, and you think candlesticks are only used in romantic dinners and birthday parties, you might want to take some of the many beginner's courses that you can find all around the internet.

If you are a beginner trader with the basic knowledge, an intermediate trader with a few years already in your back, or even an advanced one who got stuck, this book can help you move your trading abilities to the next level. It's based on simple but sound principles that are key to developing a winning strategy.

I can promise you that if you follow the advice in this book and make a serious commitment to change your trading habits, you will be in your way to become a profitable trader. It can be hard at first, but it's definitely something within your reach.

Please, if at any time, you have any questions you can write me to paul@forexlife.me or visit my blog http://forexlife.me, I'll be delighted to hear your thoughts about the book and any hurdles you might encounter in your own trading.

The blog now has a FREE video course on How to start your Journey and Become a Profitable Trader.

Please go to this website to gain access to the Free Course:

http://forexlife.me

It's important to understand that you need to make a big paradigm shift to trade profitably. Normally, in most jobs, the more you do the more you accomplish. The more you "work" the better you will do in the end. But, in trading, this common sense rule DOES NOT apply. The money you are making, or losing, is not based on how much effort you put to it, but on how well you implement a system. But, the system does its own magic by itself. The markets move by themselves, you don't really have any impact on the markets (unless you are a Central Bank moving a few hundred billions from here to there), so it's crucial to your future success to remove this self-centered approach that is needed to succeed in most other lines of work.

And, in the end after "so much work", we lose our money and our dreams of freedom. Why?

It is simply because the market has a huge component of randomness to it. A lot of what's happening is simply noise. But our minds make a big effort to make sense from all of this noise and look for patterns where there aren't any. But, there is no need to. Noise doesn't make sense. And all these hours of watching how noise does its thing are basically lost, worthless, a waste of time and better spent going to the park and watching the snails crawl in the grass.

Most people – including myself – when they begin to trade, want to be glued to the screen watching every little market move. Is it going up? Is it going down? It is forming a flag! It's touching a fib line!, I can see it!! The SMA is crossing now! I must enter!, and suddenly the market moves exactly the other way, and we ask ourselves: why? It was so clear…

So, how do we step from all this noise into making money?

How to lose $50,000 working very hard (Only to earn them back many times over)

I've been trading for over 7 years now. In those years, I have traded all: stocks, futures, Forex, E-Minis, options, I've sold puts, iron condors, spreads, and binary options; you name it, I've tried it. And I can tell you I've lost a LOT of money doing it. I have been the result of the marketers for financial information products many times and I can tell you 99.9% of what they sell is pure crap.

I've read somewhere, from the dozen of trading books I've read, that you have to pay the cost of tuition, and boy, did I pay, and dearly.

I've lost close to $50k in my first years of trading. Yes, $50,000 dollars on savings I had. And I can tell you I was not rich or any of the sort, so it did hurt a lot to lose that money. It was my life savings.

I also went to all kinds of trading material: Every time I found a new system, a new book, a new indicator, a new strategy, a new course, a newsletter, MT4, Ninja Trader, signals, robots, social trading, you name it: I bought it, tried it, and, yes, you guessed right: I failed at it. I even paid for one of this super expensive $4k trading coaches. And, yes. I failed with that, too, and lost some more money there, plus the cost of the coach.

I've lost count on how many accounts I blew, on how many Forex, commodities, stock, or options brokers I've tried; only to find that it wasn't about the broker or the markets or the news or the market makers or the indicators I was using, but the problem was within myself.

I couldn't help but wonder if it was my fault, if I was a complete dumb ass, or if the universe was against me making money. I was investing a lot of time and resources on this crazy adventure and the results were so horribly bad. I am so glad I wasn't married at that time, or had a family. The pressure would have been enormous.

I know, this sounds close to the saddest story you've ever read, but I also know it's the story of many people around who are seduced by the idea of working from home, by themselves, and earning extra fat income every month. Well, you know, in theory it's possible. The market is there, a lot of money changes hands all the time, and there is an endless stream of possibility.

You could potentially become super wealthy in a few months if you could just win all the trades you place and leverage your account like crazy.

Money moving in the billions from one place to another, huge amounts of leverage, a vast market with all the volatility of which anyone could dream, and there's even people out there making a crazy good living out of it, really.

So, I thought, If some people do it, or at least claim to do it. Then why can't I? Or, why can't you?

It took me years to answer this question. And, basically, the most accurate answer I have is:

We are asking the wrong questions to the wrong people.

For example, all these "signal providers," how is it possible that they claim to have such amazing results, but when you try to use the signals yourself somehow it's nearly impossible to achieve the same results they do. I don't know if it were me, but I was always too late or too early, or when I finally entered at the right moment suddenly I take this massive loss, and they tell you "well it's one loss after so much winning" only I never got to the "so much winning" part.

Or, all this "proven systems" that show massive trading records, it seems so easy, almost foolish not to become a millionaire in a few months, or even weeks!

Or, look at the "custom" indicators or Expert Advisors. I don't know if you've ever tried them, but somehow in real life they seem much more discretionary and hard to interpret than when you see those beautiful charts with the "model trades" where everything seems easy and clear. It's like you can almost feel your success, but somehow it never comes.

But you might know that trading is a zero sum game. It means that if someone is losing there, it means that there is some other person winning on the other side. That means that someone is actually winning! … But who? … Or how do they actually do it?

A STRANGE MEETING, A STRANGE MAN, AND SOME WINE

So, at this point: my original $60,000 dollar account, which I filled with my life savings, was close to $9,000. Yes, I've lost more than 80% of my trading capital in over a year because of my bad trading. That was money I was saving for over 10 years, so it was truly painful to see day by day how my dreams were evaporating, and the harder I tried the faster money was leaving my account.

At that time I was really struggling with my life, I was deep in to debt with my credit cards, car payments, rent, etc., and my day job was not really giving me enough money to meet my everyday needs. My girlfriend, now wife was still studying, so I really had to pay for most of the family expenses.

At some point I was about to withdraw the $9,000 I still had, take my losses, and at least pay off one of my credit cards and forget about this crazy trading adventure. This maybe would have been the most conservative and reasonable thing to do. But something happened during those days that changed my life.

In my former job I had to travel quite a bit, very extenuating working trips that drove me away from home for a few hours to a couple of days.

Anyway, back then, I was coming out from a meeting in Napa Valley, California, in an upscale hotel, and decided to sit at the bar. I ordered a sandwich; I had a couple of hours before the cab will pick me up and drive me back to the airport.

A few tables away was this older guy drinking a bottle of wine all by himself. I will not tell his real name because he is retired from the business. But we will call him Robert. Robert says hi to me, and we start chatting, separated from each other by a few tables. Finally he asks me to go over his table and invited me for a glass of wine.

He seemed a wealthy man and, as he told me back then, he was just enjoying retirement and traveling around wine countries and playing golf. He, like myself, is a big fan of red wine. So, our conversation was around that subject, and we had quite a good time together.

Robert told me that he spent most of his working years at the Deutsche Bank, which to me sounded so boring that I didn't really ask for any details. I felt my life was so much more exciting that some guy behind a desk at a bank. At the end, we did exchange email addresses and because we both liked red wine, we decided to keep in touch.

I went back home and at some point I happened to try one of the amazing wines from Mexico, I don't know if you ever tried them, but they have amazing wine down there. So, I wrote Robert and sent him a picture of Monte Xanic wine's tab.

He replied telling me that he knew everything about that wine and how much he liked it, too. But the amazing part was the signature on his email:

Robert XXXXXX

DB Forex/Futures

Senior Trading Desk Director

When he told me he worked at the DB I, never thought he'd work in this specific area of the bank!

So I decided to write him an email asking to clarify. He wrote back saying he was over 35 years in the Forex/Futures business as a trader.

That same night I wrote back telling him about all my trading frustrations, how things were so bad for me in those years, all the pain I had to endure, all the money I've lost, all the silly strategies I've tried, all the books I've read, and internet rubbish I bought, etc.

After this letter we spoke on the phone several times and, at the end, thank God for that, he agreed to mentor me for two weeks one on one and then to keep in touch with me for a few months every ,day, so I could really understand how to trade. He asked me to commit full time to this task and he agreed to show me everything he knew about trading.

For this commitment I had to give him a $6,000 token and a box of Monte Xanic wine. As you know, I didn't really have that money at the time but I didn't think about it twice, I went to the bank and asked for a loan (another loan on top of my credit cards and car payments), deposited this money to Robert, and shipped the wine bottles. A few weeks later my training started.

"You know, Paul, trading is not really what you read about in those books," he told me, and I found out he was right. Actually, after those mentoring weeks, I finally understood how especially the brokers and market makers rig everything against the retail trader. They have made a whole industry after the Internet was available and everyone could trade from home. Their industry is basically based on our bad trading. Try to go to any of the "educational" sections of the brokers and use their strategies, I'd be really surprised if you could win a buck with them. Or why do you think they give you 5 or even 1-second charts?

Who could trade with that?

Forex trading was not really conceived for individuals. It's a market for huge financial whales. But if you understand how those whales move their enormous capital, you can ride on their backs and make a lot of money. Well, a lot of money for you and me, for them is just like "small rounding errors."

The most fascinating part is that Robert taught me a way to approach the markets that worked for him for over 35 years, so it was not some fancy new thing that will stop working any moment the market changes.

So after a few months of demo trading, slowly moving to real money, hard work, and some shouting from Robert, who couldn't understand how I got to such a bad point, with so many bad trading habits, my account finally began to take off. I began making a few hundred dollars a week. I remember my first winning week was like +$134. But this number started to grow slowly but steadily.

Before I knew, I was already making 4 figures a week. My original $60,000 came back to my account in only 20 months. I was trading a bit too leveraged, I must say, but I needed desperately to feel I could stand up again and make some money out of all this.

In the third year I was already making a 6-figure income from my trading. So yes, I can tell you, it's possible to trade profitably. It is possible to start with a modest account and trade your way up to a 6- or even a 7-figure return. I will not say it's easy; it's actually quite difficult, especially because your biggest enemy in this war is not the other traders or the big banks or even the brokers, it is yourself. On the other hand, the changes you need to start to make real money are also at your reach.

Because everything depends only on you.

THE INFAMOUS "A-HA" MOMENT

In all the materials I've read before Robert's mentoring, there was all this rubbish about the "aha" moment, some sort of a revelation moment where you will understand everything that was bad in your trading and change your life, instantly.

Well, at some point I remember asking myself, "am I an idiot?" Or, why don't I get any a-ha magical moment? even though I study so hard, and even lose so much money trying to trade profitably.

I can tell you I didn't have this "aha" moment, that I've read so much about. It was more like a series of small "aha..." tiny moments. Trading is a very complex and multi variable task. That's why it can be difficult without the proper training or guidance.

At some point I started to follow my own system flawlessly and without any fear or hesitation.

Month after month, the numbers started to work in my favor. I wasn't doing any special thing, or at least I thought I wasn't, but trading became some sort of a second nature.

I know quite a bit about markets by now, and Forex currency pairs started to unfold before my eyes and I became pretty good at predicting price movements. I thought at the time; but I wasn't really predicting I was just implementing a system with an edge that, in the long run, was giving me positive results. I know it sounds complicated, but in real life the system is actually the easiest part. Realizing that you need to develop a system of your own, I mean, you don't have to re-invent the wheel, simply re-organize and fit all the knowledge to make sense to you and your personal situation.

The Right Mental Framing (or, why traders don't make money)

When I first open my real trading account with $60,000 (only to lose over $51,000 some months later), I was so proud of all that money.

For me to have all that cash just to trade was a bit of a huge self-accomplishment. Apart from that, I had another $7,000 in my savings account. So the $60k was basically all my life savings.

I had earned the money with huge effort, working for many years on my business and in day jobs. So, I was quite attached to that money … such a nice round number.

By that time, I already blew up a few real trading accounts, with some at $500 even one with $2,000. It was painful, but not such a big deal, because it was just "play" money because I haven't decided to put the bulk of my money to trade.

One of this failed accounts had a couple hundred left and I was trying a "new strategy." And, for a few weeks already, I found myself using this system that "was so good," and helping me so much, that I've already doubled the $200 and was sitting at $400 in only two weeks.

For me, this little two weeks' success was enough proof that I was ready to trade "for real." So, I deposited the $60,000 and I was ready to make a fortune in the markets.

I saw myself already in the very near future buying new houses, cars; traveling around the world ... what could go wrong? my "system" was infallible.

With the small account, I was using the maximum 100:1 leverage at that time, so I decided to take it easy and trade the $60,000 with a 2:1 ($120,000) lots.

I would be risking very little and maybe I will double my account every 6 months, or so I thought in my "easy accounting" mind. Boy, was I wrong.

But why!?? I was already doing it on my tiny $200 (now $400) account. I mean, I've read all those books about trading, and how to cut your losses and let your winners run, etc. I even bought this "Amazing" Meta Trader system that was giving me "very accurate" signals.

Yeah, sure... but.

After only 6 months, my account was in the lower $50,000's. Let alone doubling it, I was consistently and slowly losing money every week, like a car leaking oil.

Exactly what was happening? Ok, I'll tell you with one typical example from those days (some of you might feel related to this story):

My Amazing System Indicator was telling me BUY EUR/GBP, so that's what I did, I place a trade to buy a $120k lot, but after a few minutes my trade is on the red 10 pips. With a $120k lot, that is minus $120 dollars...

I mean, for me that was some good money. I could gas the tank of my car a couple of times, or take my girlfriend to the movies and then to dinner. That was hard, I didn't want to be losing $120, so I say ok: I need to wait, because my stop loss is at 30 pips (according to the Amazing System rules), so now I am waiting; every minute starts to pass slowly, very slowly.

My eyes are fixed on the screen, the candles moving randomly. And the price is still moving against me, no rebound, no retrace, only a steady bigger and bigger move against me.

Suddenly I am in the -$300 area. That was enough money for a short weekend vacation!! Man, this is painful. So I just can't stand it anymore. I am supposed to cut my loses short, right?. So I finally close the trade at a loss.

Now I can see those horrible -$327.45 (after a very bad execution from my broker and commissions expenses). And I think to myself, "ok, it was bad, but you have to learn to take loses, it's part of trading." I feel very bad about it, but I just try to be very strong and not let my emotions take control. I can tell you now that they were very much already in control by that moment and almost from the first day I began trading.

I go to the kitchen for a cup of coffee and come back after twenty minutes only to see the price went back to my entry price. So If I had stayed in the trade, now I'd be -$0. But not only that, time passes and now I see the screen in horror.

Price is going now up, more and more! If I had stayed, now I'd have +$230. Wait! Now +$315, +$456 … wow, that is really painful.

But wait!, there is always a second chance to redeem yourself: my "Amazing System" is telling me SELL USD/JPY. Ok cool. This time it will be different.

Now I'll make some serious money because this time I know better how to trade.

But look, maybe I was too crazy to bet with such a large amount last time. I mean $120k is a lot of money! I'd play it slowly now; I'd enter only a $60k lot this time.

Very good, so USD/JPY very quickly moves in my favor, it is minus a few pips now … big spike to the downside! Cool!! +20 pips for me! That's +$120!! (Remember I am now only with $60k lot) very cool. Maybe with some luck I'll recover from my last loss, maybe I'll make some money this time.

But wait, price is moving up again … it came back up a little, so now it's only +15 pips or +$90 … ok, what to do. I mean $90 is quite a good amount of money.

I could just take a few good trades like this one and I will be good for the week. Ok I'll cut it now! Closed trade +$84.77 (yes, another horrible execution from my broker), but I got some money back! Thanks God! Maybe not all, but at least I made it less painful. Maybe I am really meant to be a great trader, I greet myself.

I check some emails, read some Facebook jokes, call my girlfriend. Come back a few hours later, and … yes, I see that price has collapsed. It's like minus 65 pips from my entry point. Man!! I just had to wait, I start telling myself.

And why did I enter with half a position anyway? I mean, I could be winning $780 at this very moment!, if I would have been a little smarter, and follow the strategy I was playing, both trades could have been profitable and I would have earned $1,500!; but you know what?

I am actually in the minus $250 by now. That's awfully painful.

It took me so many losses, systems, tries, signal services, books, indicators, etc., to realize I wasn't really struggling with the markets, but actually I was struggling with myself on every trade.

And my mind was constantly playing against me. Maybe the trade was right, maybe the system was good (it wasn't, I found about how to test systems later), but I wasn't even trading the system, or executing the trades in a proper way.

I was looking at the money I was losing and gaining from a totally wrong and very damaging perspective. I was so attached to the cash I had that I couldn't bare to watch it go down or even up! Fear and greed were part of my decision-making process. Of course, it was impossible to win any money like this.

At some point, when I was in the minus $48,800 area, I realized I had to make peace with the market. I mean, by that time frustration was so big, I couldn't think of working my ass in my business again to put back $48,800 in my account only to lose it again. Earning it back with my trading appeared really impossible now.

When I was saving that money, originally, I was planning to buy a flat, at least to put a nice down payment for that purpose. Now I didn't have the money, nor the flat. And I was still renting this stupid house.

Because of my positive nature, I always tried to look at it like everything will be OK in the end. But this time I was at my breaking point. I felt like I was trapped and ready to give up.

I went for a work trip to Buenos Aires and decided to stay there for one more week, only to think of what was happening, far away from my trading station. Of course, my girlfriend was not happy about me just hanging alone there, but I felt already too embarrassed to face the situation and tell her the real reason why I couldn't just go back to my routine of losing money.

I had to understand that: first it's not personal and second: it's impossible to predict what is going to happen in the markets. So, basically, ANYTHING could happen; and it does, it really does.

How is it even possible to make money in such a treacherous environment? Is it possible at all? I can tell you: It is. It's basically a game of probability; like flipping a coin.

Let's look at this example: if you toss a coin for a few times you will not get a 50-50% probability to heads and tails. You would really need to toss it like 1,000 times to get some real accurate 50 - 50%, but imagine you set yourself the goal to toss it 1,000 times.

But, every time you are about to toss the coin, you hesitate. And, ask yourself: should I maybe not toss it this time? I think I am not using the right coin; I should try with this other coin. Stop it with your hand? Or let it go all the way to the ground? Or once the coin is in the air, you just change your mind about tossing it and grab it quickly from the air and put it back to your pocket.

That's the way most people trade. Instead of focusing on finding a good and profitable system, and then commit to apply it flawlessly every single time, they focus on every single trade, as if one trade was so important. Of course when they have three or four losing trades in a row, they simply quit and start looking for another system, they think the system is not working anymore, or they start over tweaking and trying to find relationships between facts that are not really connected.

I mean, I understand all those people very well! I was exactly like this, and I've lost such a horrendous amount of money because of that. When you are in the middle of a winning trade, it's so difficult just to wait until you reach your target, especially because many times you won't ever reach it, and then you will feel so miserable because at some point you were in profit. Or, sometimes your stop will be hit almost to the pip, and then the market will start moving in your direction for a crazy amount of pips; only this time, you were already stopped out from the trade. That's why so many people blame the brokers for "stops hunting".

TO DEMO OR NOT TO DEMO

In my mentoring time, we were only doing demo trading. If you don't have a demo account, go now and open one, I'll wait for you right here, just place the amount of money that you are planning to open your real trading account with ... ok, is it open now? Sure? Not yet? Not a problem I'll wait a little longer till you really open it ... ready? OK great!

Demo trading is very important because you will have plenty of time and infinite virtual money to lose in the time it takes you to learn to follow a system. One of the biggest disadvantages of demo is that you won't be learning to control your emotions regarding money, because we all know these are only fake dollars, or euros, or pounds. But, it's crucial to start there. Also, the brokers will give you great executions no matter what, because liquidity is infinite in the virtual money world. But, don't let that discourage you to start with a demo account, it's crucial to your success as a trader.

After you have been trading successfully for 4 - 6 months in this account, you are ready to put real money on the line, you will have enough confidence in your system and in yourself to stand a few losing trades, or you won't go crazy if suddenly you have a nice streak of winning trades.

Look, I know we all want instant results, and become wealthy before the end of the month. But the Forex markets are not the lottery, so if you really are serious about your trading, you should not skip this rule.

I was so afraid to lose more money that what I decided after the 6 months of mentoring and demo trading successfully was to let alone my "real" account that was standing at some $9k and start trading with one of my old accounts that had some $100 that I could barely trade because the margin was so tight. The great thing about that tiny account is that I didn't really care about the money, only the system, because it wouldn't have hurt much to lose $100. So, my mind was focused on executing the strategy right to see how it worked with real money, even if it was such a tiny amount.

After only a few weeks my account was in the $200's, so I decided I'd deposit from my "big" account another $200, so I had $400 to trade. Then, when I was at $800, I moved another $800 from the big account. And so I did until I depleted my old account. It was a renovating process. It didn't last very long, a few months. But it completely drove my mind from the money-worrying problem I had. Because I always had a 50% cushion I could lose and still be the same as I was before my last deposit. And, also because for a while I was worrying to gain and lose only a few bucks, so it wasn't really worrying at all.

If you are hurt from past horrible trading history like I was, you can try my strategy, starting with only a few hundreds and deposit more once you get to a certain threshold, but only after you have demo for a while and feel confident about your system.

WHY TRADE THE FOREX MARKETS

The Forex markets are a huge, highly liquid, and decentralized market. What does that mean? It means there is not an exchange (like in the stock market) or any single institution that is responsible for what and how it is traded. It's an enormous Over the Counter market where banks and other big institutions just trade currency pairs for the price that "seems" right to the market. In other words, they sell to the highest bidder and buy from the lowest offer.

Compared to the apparently large $22.4 billion a day volume of the New York Stock Exchange, the foreign exchange market becomes absolutely enormous with its $5 TRILLION a day trade volume. That gives you a great advantage when trying to fill a trade, there will be enough liquidity to fill even big positions instantly, no matter if you want to go short or long.

Because it's mostly unregulated, it has many great qualities. For example, the barrier to entry is basically nonexistent. You can open a Forex account with a few dollars, some brokers will let you open it with as little as $20. Compare that with the minimum $25,000 you need to day trade in the stock exchange markets.

Although the U.S. government has enforced leverage rules (maximum 50:1 in Majors) and some other nonsense, like the FIFO rule (some regulation that forces you to close your positions beginning from your oldest position to your newest, if you have many in the same pair), the world is full of brokers who will give you massive leverage, even 1,000:1 (not that anyone should trade with such a crazy amount of leverage), allow you hedging, don't care what position you close or open first, or let you withdraw and deposit your money via Paypal or Moneybookers or even Bitcoin.

Of course, with all this freedom there is the chance to find yourself with very bad and dishonest people who are only trying to part you from your money (everyone is but it's fair if it's within the rules because that way you are allowed to take other traders money, too). But, with a bit of research, you can find a reputable broker that is regulated in it's country of origin, has good reviews, and has decent spreads and/or commissions. Just work a little and put the effort to find the right one for you.

Because of it's global use, the Forex market is open 24 hours a day from, Monday morning in New Zealand to Friday afternoon in NY. So, you don't depend on business hours and you can adapt your trading to your sleeping habits, your time zone, and, most of all, you will not wake up the next morning to find huge gaps in the after-hours markets – like in the equities markets where it's so common, because your stops and take profits will be in place working also 24 hours a day.

There is no middle man, less commissions, less cost of trading, all of this because the brokers normally use electronic instant filing systems and deal directly with liquidity providers like big banks, they can give you crazy cheap transaction costs compared with other markets like the futures market or the stock exchanges. For only a few dollars' worth of spread, you can trade in the tenths, hundreds of thousands, or even millions, making use of leverage and low trading costs.

Leverage is a way to trade the markets effectively without having big accounts. You know that currency exchange rates move in such a small fractions of points that to make money trading, let's say buying $1,000 of EUR/USD at 1.1294 and then sell it to 1.1344, a sad $5 bucks win, minus spread and commissions.

So, the brokers came with the solution of lending you the ability to enter a position bigger than what you have to a ratio of your choice. Depending on the broker, it can be 50:1, 100:1, 400:1, and more. So, your original $1,000 could control $100,000 in a 100:1 account; in that case, instead of your $5 winning trade you would be sitting in a $500 win, making a 50% winning on your capital in a single small trade.

Of course, leverage works both ways, so it must be used wisely and conservatively, it should always be another component of your strategy. Consider that if your account allows you a maximum 100:1 leverage, it doesn't mean that you need to trade using all of the leverage, or even most of it. Sometimes 2:1 or 5:1 is more than enough to make good money.

When I was first starting to trade, I was looking for the button to lower the leverage, because I've read somewhere that it was dangerous to trade with too much leverage, and found I could only lower it to a minimum of 50:1 in my brokerage account. I was quite angry and even contacted customer support about this issue. Somehow I didn't see that I could just enter a smaller position and disregard of my maximum leverage setting. It's basic, but can confuse novice traders.

If you ever traded penny stocks, you know there is always the possibility of some big pockets to corner the particular stock you are trading. They could literally take it to the moon and then make it crash to the ground willingly, and if you are in the wrong side you can get really hurt. The Forex markets can't be cornered because they are so enormous; however, Central Banks and some other government institutions can introduce wild volatility effects, so be careful when big news come out. However, a currency, especially a major one, can never go to zero, or lose 95% of it's value, like many companies do on a regular basis.

BASICS OF TRADING

These are very basic technical concepts. If you are reading this book, I am sure you are familiar with them. Just take a quick glance so we know we are speaking about the same concepts when we talk about specific strategies later in the book.

My strategies are not constructed around complicated indicators or many technical tools, just the very basic and most powerful ones. I believe you don't need to have a "spaghetti" chart to trade profitably; on the contrary, it will distract you from the price action and give you mostly irrelevant information, trying to make sense from simple and plain noise.

Trends and Ranges

Markets can only do two things: range bound or trend. That means that whether they are trapped in a smaller zone going up and down without breaking this zone, or they can trend, meaning they go constantly in the same direction, further and further: higher and higher or lower and lower.

However, markets don't go in a straight line. They tend to move a bit in one direction then retrace and then a bit further, then abruptly in one direction, then pause again, retrace a bit, and so on. Sometimes the movement can seem random, but if you see it from a longer time frame, things can get much clearer.

A Bullish trend is when the market goes higher and higher, making higher highs and higher lows.

A Bearish trend is when the market goes lower and lower, making lower highs and lower lows.

SUPPORT AND RESISTANCE

Support is a horizontal line, the "floor" where price action appears to stop and rebound higher or stay around it for some time without crossing it in a definitive way, making it a psychological barrier for traders. Thus it is something significant when it's finally broken.

Resistance is a horizontal line, the "roof" where price action appears to stop and rebound lower or stay around it for some time without crossing it in a definitive way, making it a psychological barrier for traders. Thus it is something significant when it's finally broken.

When a Support zone is finally broken and price moves definitely lower, this former support normally becomes resistance.

When a Resistance zone is finally broken and price moves definitely higher, this former resistance normally becomes support.

Don't worry if you don't know exactly where to place support and resistance, every trader place them a bit different, they should be taken more like zones than exact points.

In all my trading strategies, I never plot support and resistance in lower time frames; the most useful are daily and weekly, they are the most significant and thus the easier to use for technical trading.

To plot resistance in a 1-hour chart or 4-hour chart, in my opinion, is useless because the bigger money (banks, hedge funds) don't move real money in the lower time frames, and they are the ones really making and affecting the markets.

OK, here's why you started reading the book in the first place…

Let's talk about strategies

The strategies described in this book were developed by me after several months of coaching and testing. They are statistically solid and can bring great results, depending on how deeply you understand them and how well you execute them. That doesn't mean they will always give you winning trades or that you will have a 100% rate of success using them. You are welcome to use them as they are or to adapt them to your own trading style.

I wanted to show you sample ideas for different types of trading, depending on your personality, your current situation, and how much you want to be involved in the markets. They should be seen as a starting point for you to develop your own strategy that suits you better. There is no one strategy that will serve everyone because all of us have different needs and expectations.

The idea is to prove that a winning strategy by no means has to be complicated or hard to understand. On the contrary, I believe that a good strategy should be simple and have as little parameters as possible to make it effective, easy to focus, and easy to measure.

If you keep a trading journal, after every single trade you make you will be able to achieve much better results in the long term, and also understand better what's working, what's not working, and how to avoid mistakes.

If you want to download a .xls file with the parameters to keep a journal, you can download one at my blog post http://www.forexlife.me/?p=100 in there you will find a link for the download.

Position trading Strategy "Big Bulls and Bears"

If you are a person who doesn't have the time to keep watching the screen all day, or who wants to focus on other things in life, or maybe psychologically it's too hard for you to just look at the market all time (like happened to me many times), I'll show you a very simple strategy that will allow you to collect income in a very regular and simple way.

With this strategy, you will not have a lot of trades, maybe one or two every month, but a big number of them will be profitable and they will allow you to collect a nice stream of income.

Step 1: Check the markets EVERY weekend, in a WEEKLY CHART, you have plenty of time after the market is closed on Friday afternoon, but you need to do it before the market reopens on Monday, or Sunday, depending on your time zone.

Step 2: You will look for this candlestick formations, and this formation ONLY in any pairs you want to trade, I wouldn't limit myself here, the more the merrier. Just try to avoid the big spread pairs:

Engulfing Candles - an engulfing candle looks basically like this,

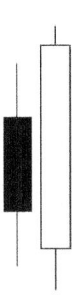

Please note that the high and the low of the last candle are higher than the high and the low of the previous candle, if they are the same height at either one of the extremes, they are not valid engulfing candles.

Bullish Engulfing Candles: These are candles that close higher than they open, and they show high amount of bullish power. They are a possible signal to go long.

Bearish engulfing: These are candles that close lower than they open, and they show high amount of bearish power. They are a possible signal to go short.

Step 3: Look for important areas of resistance and support or continuation movements in case the trend is very clear.

Step 4: Place your stop at the top or bottom of the engulfing candle, depending if it's a long or short trade.

Step 5: Depending on the distance from the entry to the stop, you will determine your risk, thus your position size. If you have a 200 pips distance to the stop loss and you are risking, let's say, $400 per trade, your position size should be $20,000.

Step 6: Place your stop entry a few pips above or below the high or the low of the engulfing candle, depending if it's a bullish or a bearish trade.

Step 7: Move to break even after the price has gone 50% of the size of the engulfing bar in your direction, in this example: 100 pips.

Step 8: For the quickest and safest profit, exit after a 150% move of the size of the candle in your direction, i.e., 300 pips. Another option will be to keep trailing every 100 pips to increase your Risk-to-Reward Ratio. Yet another option is to find support and resistance levels and trail according to those lines. There's no right or wrong way to do it, just different possibilities for your personal taste and objectives.

If you trail, you will have some frustrating break evens, but you will also hit crazy home runs, like a huge EUR/JPY movement I was able to trade for over 1,200 pips a few months ago. If you don't trail and go directly for the 150% target price, you will have a bigger amount of winning trades, but in smaller profit sizes each.

I will put a few sample trades, although they're trades I did take and made money, I will cherry pick them to show you how they should look. It doesn't mean that every trade I picked was a massive winner, but I think after watching these trades you will be able to take a look at the charts and find some for yourself and even back test easily with different position sizing and trailing or target methods you might plan to use, and thus fine tune your own strategy to your liking.

Here's an example from EUR/GBP last week of October 2013

Here's how this trade unfolded

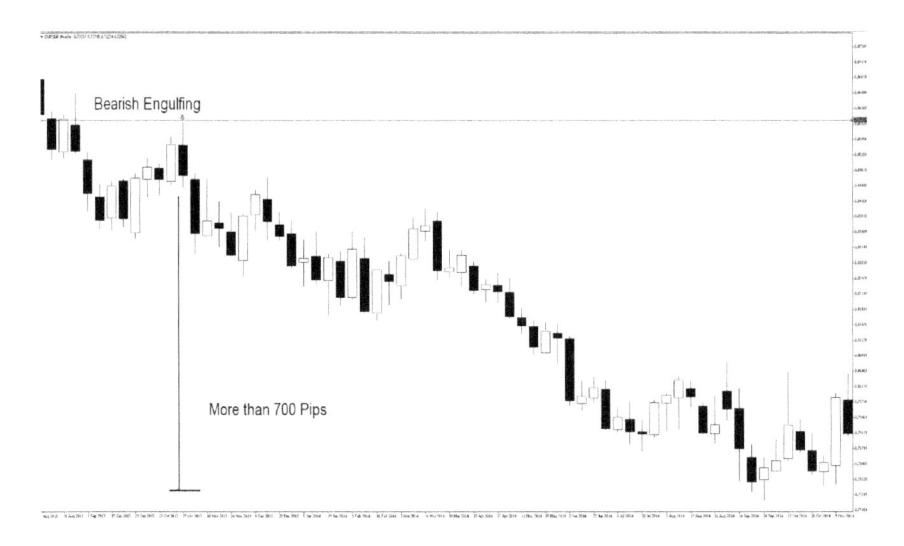

Bearish Engulfing

More than 700 Pips

Depending on your particular strategy you could have ride this enormous trend or simply make your 150% profit; maybe breakeven or something in between, but this sample demonstrates the power of these setups to anticipate long trends.

Here's an example from the USD/CAD on the third week of July 2012

Bearish Engulfing

Support

This is a clear continuation trend trade, we can see that the support /

resistance line has become one or the other several times. However we see a clear sign (our Bearish Engulfing Candle) to go short on this important area.

The same trade setup, a little closer.

This is how the trade unfolded:

This trade had a big potential for trailing and capture a good part of the move.

Here's another trade

This a EUR/JPY chart from a trade I did December 2014. As you can see, the Relevant Resistance was way back in 2008 and 2007; that's why the chart has so much zoom back. However, when prices are reaching new highs all the time, you have to go back many years to see how prices was reacting back then at those levels. It's amazing how they are still valid even so many years later.

Here's a view of the setup in a closer look, and how it unfolds:

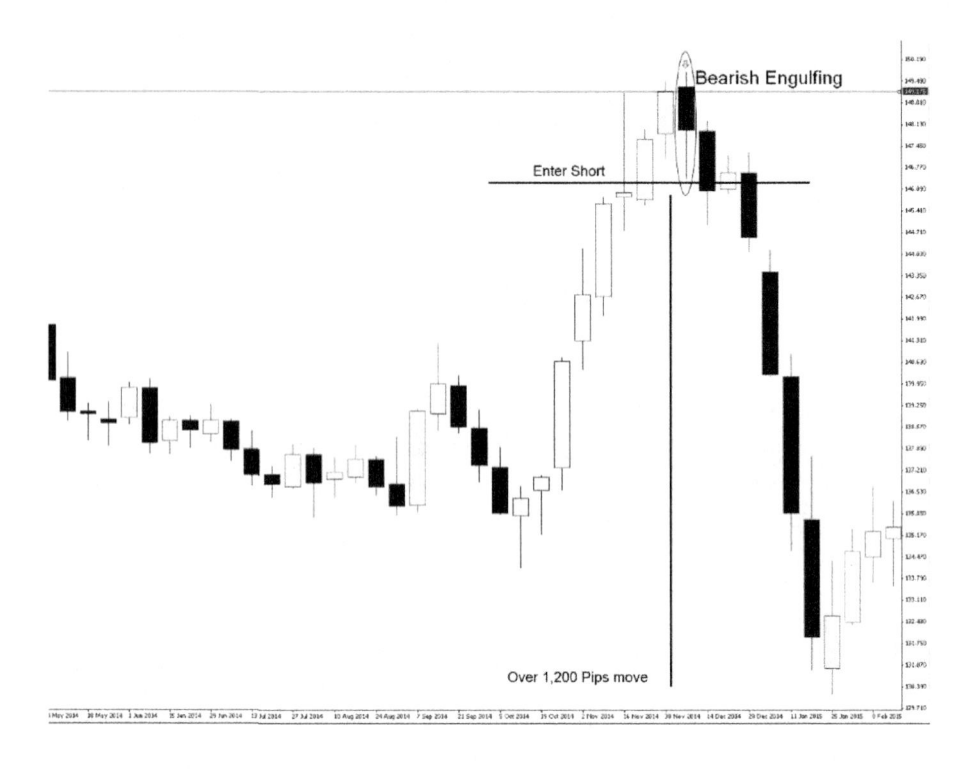

This is what we pray for in this strategy, a clean 1,200 pips move, in only 6 weeks! It was a nice way to start 2015.

As you can see, these trades can span from a few weeks to several months, but there are always some good opportunities out there to enter more trades, I normally don't limit myself to only one single trade at the time, but divide my risk to be able to trade two or even three trades at the same time.

It's important to consider that if you, for example, are already in a USD/JPY trade, to enter another USD or JPY related trade will be like doubling your risk in the same trade. Although they will not move in the exact same fashion, they will be correlated and mostly have the same overall movement.

A Swing Trading Strategy

The strategy we will use for Swing Trading is quite similar to the Position Trading, we will be looking for the same pattern on the daily charts (Engulfing Candles). Although with a few particularities:

We will only enter trades in the direction of the overall trend in the daily chart, at relevant support and resistance levels. If the trend is not clear, we can enter in a range trade at either side of the range.

We will normally wait for a retracement of the main direction to enter the trades in the direction of the trend. Or when a relevant support and resistance level is broken with an Engulfing Candle.

Place a pending order 4 - 6 pips above or below the bullish or bearish candle. Place the stop order above or below the engulfing candle.

Move to break even after the next minor resistance or support is passed.

Trail every three candles or target a relevant support or resistance.

This strategy will normally give you a 1 - 3 trades a week, it's very important that you check the markets every day after the NY session is over, also try to look for a broker who gives you NY closing charts. Although there's is not an official session for the Forex markets, NY closing charts will put you closer to what professional futures traders view.

You can trade all the pairs that you like, just try to avoid the big spread pairs; they will work too (I mean USD/TRY or EUR/NOK, or similar) but you will pay a higher price for trading them.

EUR/CAD Trade from February 2015

Here we have a tight range and a big Bearish Engulfing Candle at one of the extremes. Although we could have entered a stop sell order a few pips bellow our bearish candle for the next session, and place our stop above the high of the Bearish Engulfing Candle.

This is how the trade unfolded:

Depending on your exit strategy you could have banked between 200 and 600 pips in two or three weeks.

Here's an example of a trade in the NZD/JPY from February 2014

As you can see there was a clear uptrend (higher highs and higher lows) that retraced to an important support level and it was there when the Bullish Engulfing Candle formed, which gave us the clue that the trend will continue it's course. This is how the trade unfolded:

Next is an example of the USD/CAD from July 2012, as you can see the downtrend was starting to resume it's move and we've got a Big Bearish Engulfing Candle right at the relevant Support that was broken and thus became resistance.

Once again, the bearish engulfing candle was the beginning of a nice move that drove the markets for more than 400 pips. Of course it's hard to catch the entire swing, but disregard of your exit strategy, most likely you would have been able to harvest quite a few pips from this trade, if you'd have been there to trade it.

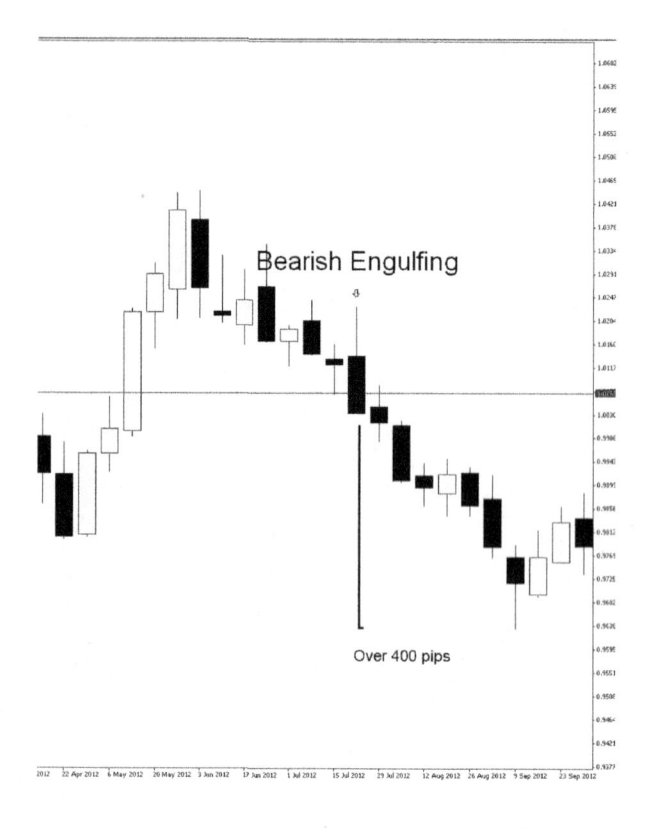

Bearish Engulfing

Over 400 pips

A Scalping Strategy

Scalping is a trading technique focused on going in and out of the markets in periods of a few minutes to a few hours. It's the most intensive, time consuming, and mentally challenging environment for trading.

I wouldn't recommend that you scalp unless you already have significant experience and success trading the longer timeframes. You will be tested to the limit in this kind of trading and if you go directly to scalp without proper preparation and training, very likely you will lose a lot of money before you can become profitable. That's why you should start trading demo at first with this strategy even if you are already making money in the longer timeframes, until you feel comfortable and you have mastered the strategy.

It's also important to limit your leverage because you will be entering and exiting the markets very often and:

a) You can make mistakes (we all do)

b) You will be making money from the bulk of your trades, they can add up in the month to 50 or even 100, so don't focus on every trade but rather on implementing the strategy correctly.

Using a broker with low spreads and NO commission, a normal

commission can be around $2.50 for every side. That means $5.00 for every trade per mini lot. If you make 100 trades a month, you will need to earn an extra $500 only to break even for every $10k lot you trade.

The other caveat of this strategy is that you can only trade in the highest volatility times of the day. If you live in Canada, for example, the London open will be very late at night for you, so maybe you will decide to trade only the NY open.

This is a trend following strategy, but we will wait for the retracements to enter only in the direction of the daily trend. You can expect to have between 2 - 5 trades for every pair every day. Although in rare occasions the setup could not appear for the whole session. So patience is also a key element in this strategy.

The strategy seems a bit complicated at first, if detailed step by step, but make an effort to understand it overall and in the samples you'll find below it will become much clearer.

For clarity sake, in the rules we will imply a bullish overall trend and a bullish trade, for bearish markets you only need to invert the rules.

Check the news calendar. If you have a significant event this day, avoid the temptation and simply don't trade two or three hours after and before the event. You can check into sites like fxstreet.com, the news calendar, only take in account the most important events. In Fxstreet they are marked with a red "!!!" sign. In the NFP Friday it's better not to trade at all.

Trade only in the busiest hours of the day, London session and NY session.

Find one to four pairs, the ones with the lowest spreads, normally the Majors (EURUSD, USDJPY, USDCAD, AUDUSD, NZDUSD, GBPUSD). Start with one or two pairs until you feel comfortable with the strategy.

Check the overall trend in the daily charts and only trade in that direction. If the pair looks very choppy and it's hard to define a range or a trend, it is better to change pairs.

Draw horizontal lines in the main resistance and support areas in the daily chart.

Plot a 20, 0 Bollinger band in a 5-minute candlestick chart. (Why Bollinger Bands? Well, they are standard in every trading platform, and basically what we need is a sign of the retracement to be ending, so it really could be Keltner channels or Fibos, Pivots, or whatever you feel more comfortable with, but I had good experience using the Bollinger Bands)

If the overall trend is up, you will look for a setup to enter a long pending order when the retracement has pierced the edge of the lower channel in the Bollinger Bands.

If the price is range bounding, wait for a breakout in from the range to start looking for setups.

Wait for a bullish candle to appear and enter a pending long order if the price breaks through the last bullish candle high.

If price don't hit your entry, wait for the next bullish candle after price has pierced the lower Bollinger Band line and enter a stop order again.

Place your stop above the significant low of the last few candles.

Move to break even after 10 pips.

Let it ride using the previous third bar low as a trailing stop, or alternatively you can exit when the price reaches a significant support or resistance.

In this strategy you could also go for a fix amount of pips like 10 or 20 pips. I've found that 20 pips is a constant hit, so you could go for 20 pips if you don't want to have so many break even trades and increase your winning ratio to a very high level. Of course you will miss the bigger swings.

Like with all the strategies, you need to adapt your exits to your own trading needs and personality.

Ok, so here's a sample trade step by step to make it perfectly clear.

Here's a daily chart for the EUR/USD on March 31, 2015; the trend is clearly down in the daily charts. So, we will start to look for bearish trades.

Now we will see how the market is doing early in the morning 8:00 am NY time, right when the markets open.

This is a 5 minutes candlestick chart with a 20, 2 Bollinger Band indicator from early morning of March 31, 2015.

The red vertical line is the session's open. After this line we can see the price moving right into the upper channel line and above it. That's where we start looking for a bearish candle. This candle comes right after the fourth bullish candle. We can enter our entry stop (short order) and place our stop above this bearish candle.

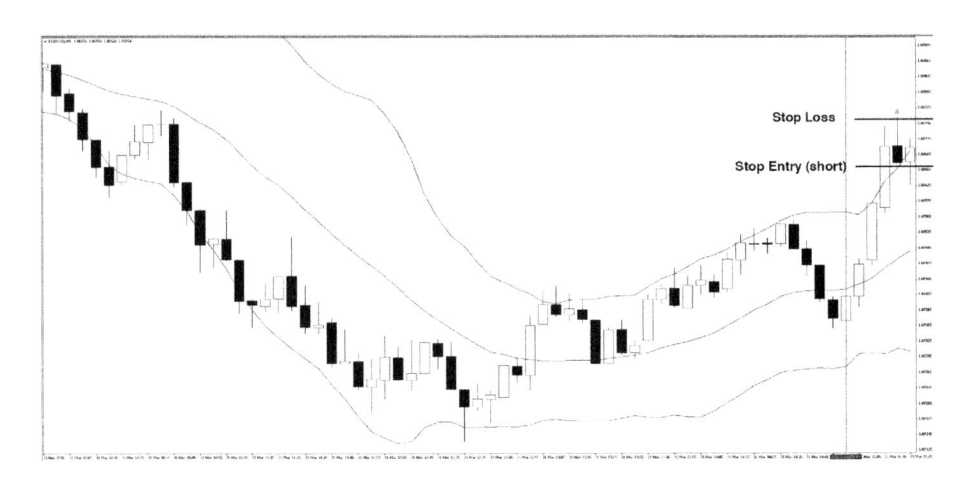

A candle later we were already in the trade. Let's see how things unfolded.

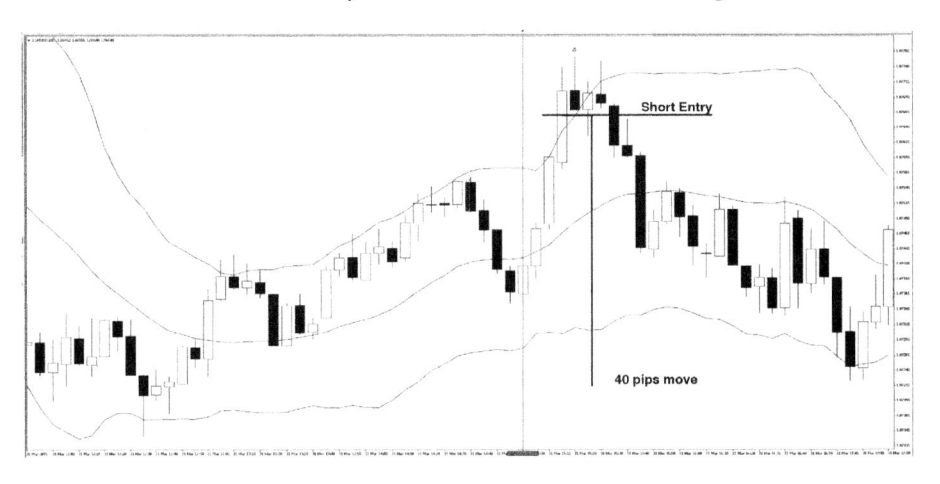

As you can see there was a 40 pips move. Depending on our exit strategy we could have got at least 10 pips or more.

This would be the next trade for the same day March 31, 2015. After our last trade we wait for the price to get back and pierce the upper Bollinger Band, When that happens we wait for a bearish candle and place our stop short entry don't forget to place your stop above this bearish candle.

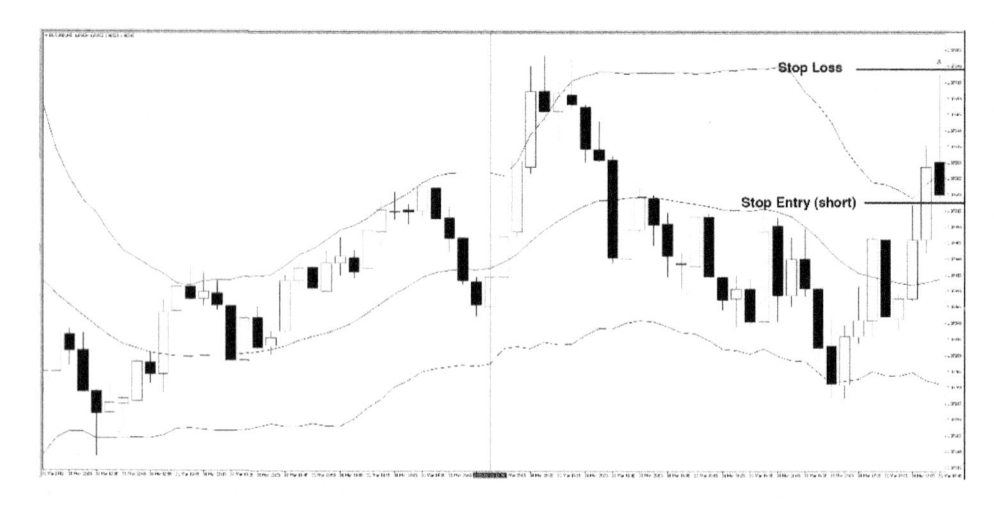

Right after we entered our pending order the trade triggers and we are in again.
As you can see, prices moves for at least 20 pips in our favor before any significant retrace.

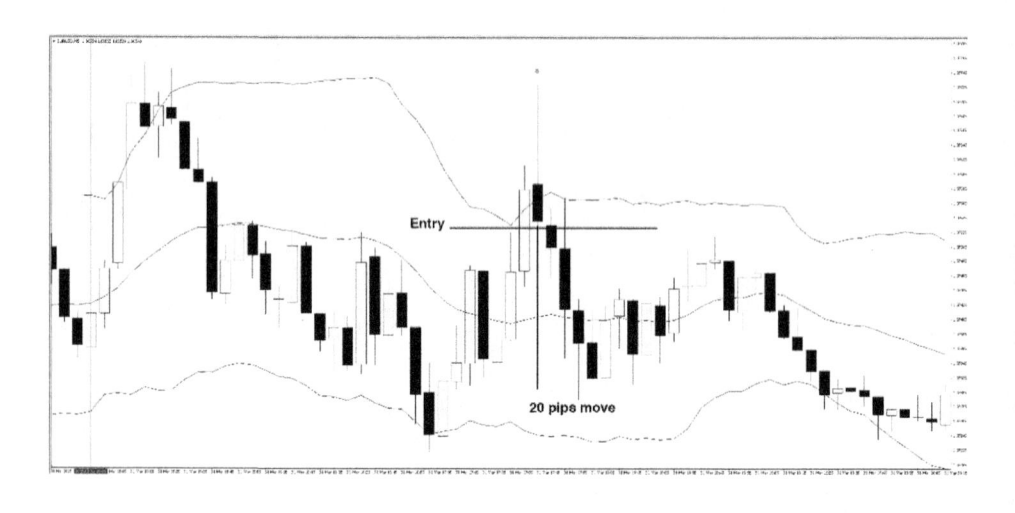

If you just open a chart from today or yesterday or the day before and look for the setup, most likely you will find valid trades. Of course, not all of them are winners, but it's a high probability, easy to follow setup for scalping.

I seriously recommend to you, if you are willing to scalp, to first back test for at least a few months back and then, to try demo to see how you react to real time conditions before committing any money to this strategy.

You'll need some practice to understand how the strategy works in different market conditions, please use your fake dollars for this practice!

The Unexpected "Holy Grail" of Trading, or How to Calculate Your Position Size

Position size is the single most crucial element in your trading, more than a correct entry or a correct stop. More than any strategy or self-psychological control ability, position size can make or break your trading career. So don't take it for granted because it is truly the "holy grail" of trading.

After trading for four to six months in the demo account, and keeping a detailed journal, you should be able to know quite well the expectancy of your system.

You need to find out and have a clear knowledge about the following ratios:

Average Risk /Reward Ratio - How much you normally risk to win how much, this number is expressed as:

1:1 if, for example to win 10 pips you risk 10 pips.

2:1 could be that to win 50 pips you risk 25

3:1 could be that to win 90 pips you risk 30

And so on

1:2 will be that you risk 40 pips to make 20 pips

The next important number to take into account is the percentage of winning trades. You could be winning only 60% of your trades, or even 30%, and still be successful. So, to win in the Forex markets it doesn't mean that you win all the individual trades, maybe even lose most of them, and in some systems you can mostly lose in a per-trade basis and still be making a good amount of money.

Once you have your winning rate and your Average Risk / Reward Ratio, you can calculate how big your position should be, depending on your risk tolerance, it has to be a number that is coherent with your risk / reward ratio and your winning ratio.

Professional traders normally risk .5% to 1% of course they manage bigger amounts of money. Most professional traders say that any account under $100k is not worth the time and effort.

For us, the retail traders, we may not have the luck to start with a $100k account, but the nice part is that we can build it up if we keep focus and are very disciplined, and take it all the way to $100k and more.

So, back to our calculations: Let's say that you know that your system is right 60% of the times and your risk/reward is 2:1, meaning that you normally risk 20 pips to gain 40 pips. In other words, for every 100 trades, you will win in average 240 pips and lose 80, leaving you with around 1,600 pips.

Now let's explore scenarios on how big your position size could be. Let's say that you have a $10,000 account. You decide to try with a risk of 1% per every trade. That will mean that 20 pips should account for 1% of your total account, in this case $100, so your position size has to be $50,000. So normally you will risk 1%, or $100, to make $200. After a whole round of 100 trades, you should have gained $8,000 if you kept your risk locked in 1% of $10,000.

Thanks to your demo trading journal, you'll also know how long you will take to make this 100 trades, so you can mostly know how much money you will make in a certain amount of time. If, for example, you are scalping 50 trades a month, that will mean that on average you will be making 40% of capital gains every month. Especially if you're scalping, you should take into account commissions and spreads because they will impact your account too. Luckily, you have your journal to find out what these numbers are.

You have to be aware that you could get a losing streak of a few trades in a row (in your detailed journal you must figure out what was your worst losing streak and take it as a standard possibility). If, for example, you had 6 losing trades in a row, that will leave you suddenly with - 120 pips. Your position sizing should be sensible to this fact, so your account doesn't suffer a dramatic loss from a normal event in your system.

In the case of a $10,000 account and risk of 1%, you can find yourself with minus $600 or $9,400, and, because of your 2:1 ratio, you can also know that with 3 winning trades you will recoup your loses. In the case of 1% to lose $600 from a $10k is not nice but far from catastrophic.

 Depending on your expectancy rates and your personal tolerance to risk, you can tweak this number to whatever suits you best. However, risking more than 5% in every trade is normally considered dangerous. Let's say you have this 6 losing trades in a row, or even a 10-in-a-row event, that can maybe happen every 1 or 2 years in the normal life of your system. If you are risking 5%, or $500 in your $10,000 account, you will find yourself with only $5,000, and loss of 50% of your capital. That starts to be catastrophic. On the other hand, if you'd be risking only 1%, you will sit in a -$1,000 loss. It will be tough to make it back, but it shouldn't be a problem after a few weeks of focused trading.

Yes, it sounds compelling to risk a big amount, especially if you are on a winning streak. You could easily double your account in a few weeks, but take in account that your system also has losing streaks into which you will certainly fall. Don't let them be the end of your trading career.

Sometimes your system is not set in exact stops, but it's different in every case because you put your stop above some event like a recent high or a resistance level. In that case, you only need to calculate your position size according to that stop.

For example: if you want to risk 1% of $10k, or $100. and your stop is set to 34 pips, then 34 pips should equal $100 or 100/34 x 10,000 = $29,411. Depending on your broker, sometimes you can't trade such an exact position. So you can use what's closer, in this case $29k or $30k.

If you are risking 2% of your $10k account, or $200 in this case, your formula will be 200/34 x 10,000 = 58,823

The formula will be:

Your risk amount in $ / the amount of pips your stop is set to x 10,000

The Black Swans

There's a factor to consider in trading that could impact so greatly your account that it can make you a huge amount of money in one day or decimate your account to rags.

They are the Black Swan events (using the term coined by Nassim Taleb in his book by the same name).

I will put as an example: the very recent Swiss Franc event. The Central Bank of Switzerland wanted to keep its currency (the Swiss franc) in a tight range with the euro, only because people were moving so much money to Switzerland that the franc was quickly appreciating, making it hard for Swiss companies to make a profit outside of their country because everything was getting so much expensive in Switzerland. It was affecting tourism and small businesses because people from Switzerland will just cross the borders to a bordering country to buy everything they needed, from groceries to gasoline.

So the Central Bank decided to buy euros and sell francs every time the currency tried to move higher (in huge amounts). In the beginning, the plan seemed to work and things were kept in check for a long time. Of course, even Central Banks have only a certain amount of money they can count on. So, after several years of this policy, one day they found out that they could no longer enforce this policy and decided to stop buying euros, without any warning or exit plan or anything, just stop buying.

In an instant all the CHF (Swiss franc) related pairs went nuts. For example, the USDCHF (US dollar / Swiss franc) went down by around 1,900 pips in a single day, well, actually, in a few minutes. This had tremendous impact in the Forex markets; suddenly all the leveraged positions the brokers were holding exploded and became like an atom bomb.

The problem is that when these events happen, markets go so crazy that even stops and take profits can't be filled, there are so many orders to get out of the trades that there is simply not enough liquidity, or the markets move so fast that it's impossible to honor simple stop losses or take profits orders.

In our example of a $10k account, let's say you were in the USD/CHF risking 3%, or $300 from a 20 pips loss, that would have make you hold a $150,000 position. If you'd have been in the right side of the trade, suddenly you would have shown a +$21,850 profit or $31,850 as a total capital.

On the other hand, if you would have been on the wrong side of the trade, your account will be -$11,850 in debit!!

In the terms and conditions of the brokerage accounts they have a policy to take you out before you are in red numbers, but in this case there was no time or chance to do it. So, brokers had to face millions of dollars in losses they couldn't collect from clients. Even big established brokers had problems and some had to file for bankruptcy.

This story is to illustrate the rare events that happen in the market every once in a while; it doesn't matter how much you prepare, they do happen. Before the CHF event, there was the 2008 crisis, or 9/11, or Katrina.

The only thing you can do to protect from these events is to:

ALWAYS trade with a stop loss, no matter what; not doing so is like jumping from the plane without a parachute.

After a winning streak from your normal trading, maybe if you double your account, or if you are up 50% or whatever number suits you, withdraw some money from your Forex account into your bank or change it to gold or stocks or whatever you like, to protect you from catastrophic events and/or problems the brokers might have.

The most important one: don't trade your rent money, or the money you need to live. Be responsible about this and you will have much less pressure on your shoulders. This will give you a much better chance to trade right and be focused and professional about your trading.

THE IMPORTANCE OF HAVING A TRADING PLAN

The following chapter is a post from my blog forexlife.me, I decided to include it in the book since I believe it speaks a very important subject on Forex trading many times neglected, that can be the difference between winning and losing in the markets: the importance of having a great trading plan.

In 1815, Napoleon was back in power and back in business after his escape from forced exile.

Every leader in Europe was well aware that if Napoleon would get strong again, blood will run through Europe once more and empires will fall to his feet again.

Therefore Everyone who could, sent his army to defeat the *Enfant Terrible*: The United Kingdom, Russia, Austria, Netherlands, Belgium and Prussia mobilized armies to defeat Napoleon, forming the Seventh Coalition.

However outnumbered, Napoleon had a much stronger leadership and a better equipped and trained army. Knowing that his enemies were approaching he decided to take the upper hand and attack first.

Napoleon

His first strategic move was to defeat the Prusian leader Prince Blücher so he could avoid him to join the Duke of Wellington's army which would have made a huge army too big for Napoleon to defeat; he fought Blücher and defeated his army on June 16 at the Battle of Ligny.

The Prussian Leader had basically amateurs and volunteers for soldiers, his artillery was incomplete and reorganizing; the Cavalry and infantry were mostly unequipped and undertrained. However his leaders and himself were well prepared, they had a very strong line of command and had a plan to strictly follow in case things went wrong, which they did.

At the first sign of a losing battle; finding the help of the Duke of Wellington, his main ally, well a day away, and seeing the much stronger French army and tactics, the Prussians strategy was to simply retreat, cutting their losses short, to a safer spot on the north, in a counterintuitive move to still stay close to the Duke of Wellington in case they needed to help each other later on.

Napoleon felt so empowered because of this victory that simply didn't give enough attention to the Prussians retreat, thinking that they will just flee back home to a stronger position. He did send a small army to pursue them but already one day too late to reach tem and stop their regrouping at the north.

At this point Napoleon thought that his plan of separating the Duke of Wellington Army and the Prussian Army was already a success. Pursuing the Duke of Wellington, who was retreating after the defeat of the Prussians, all the way back to Waterloo one step closer to the sea, where Napoleon was expecting to drive the Brits and force them back to Britain.

The Duke of Wellington was commanding the combined forces from the United Kingdom, Netherlands and Belgium. However bigger in numbers, they were weaker compared to the more prepared and loyal armies of

Napoleon which were veterans of many battles and were following Napoleon blindly and even fanatically.

The Duke of Wellington chose a good spot to fight (Waterloo) and did a good job holding Napoleon's forces throughout the day forcing heavy losses on both sides.

If you could have seen the battle from above, one could have see that, although with a great effort, Napoleon was much closer to the victory. If he had followed a detailed plan, most likely Napoleon would have never let the Prussians escape after the defeat.

Maybe he wouldn't have attacked a stronger post like Waterloo were heavy loses were foreseeable because it was a good place to defend and a hard one to attack.

He was so excited about his winnings that he simply thought of himself as invincible and decided to march and fight the Duke of Wellington, although there were a few factors that were not 100% in his favor in this attack.

When things were definitely leaning towards Napoleon the Duke of Wellington famously said: "Night or the Prussians must come". To his luck, the Prussians had time to regroup and were marching towards Napoleon's left flank. The decimated French forces that had already fought all day couldn't stop the Prussians and eventually, Napoleon's left flank retreated and blocked the right flank's possible way of retreat.

With the confusion reigning in the French troops and without a good retreat plan; Napoleon never thought he could lose a battle so he simply didn't think what to do in case something went wrong, Napoleon's Army was defeated at the Battle of Waterloo on Sunday, 18 June 1815, marking his fall from power and his last days as the Commander and leader of the French.

Prince Leberecht von Blücher

War and Forex Trading are quite similar in many ways. We, as retail traders are more like the Prince Blücher fighting Napoleon. We have less capital (a smaller, less capable army) and we don't have many allies to come to our help in case we guess the price direction wrong. However we can choose what battles to fight and how to fight them; that's our ONLY advantage and the one thing we can plan and do right as traders.

If you feel yourself like Napoleon because you had a few winning trades and stop following your own plan and rules, most likely you will make a mistake and your enemies will take advantage of it and destroy you.

In the long run The Market will only reward disciplined and humble traders who understand their strengths and plan for their limitations and know what to do in case things go wrong.

To make a trading plan we must understand a few factors that are key to our success as traders:

1. Position sizing – How big our position will be
2. Stop Loss – How much we are willing to lose in every trade in a percentage basis
3. Take profit – when are we planning to go out, how much are we expecting to win in case things go our way. Do we intend to trail stops? Do we have a fixed take profit? Should we close half of our position at a predefined point and let the other half run?

Together with the specific setups we expect to find in the markets in order to enter the trades and "engage in battle".

This would be an example of a scalp-trading plan:

- I will only trade the NY Session
- I will close any open trades left before the NY session closes
- I will not trade around important news events like the NFP
- I will only trade pairs that are trending

- I will only trade pairs that offer a spread of 5 pips or less
- My position sizing will limit my loses to 2% of my capital every time
- I will go for setups that provide at least a 2:1 opportunity
- I will move my s/l to break even when prices moves 50% of the desired move
- I will only enter the markets if my setup coincides with the overall trend
- I will enter only if so and so indicators and so and so setups are telling me to enter (here is where you state your trading system for finding entry setups)
- I will enter a maximum of 5 trades a day no matter what
- I will stop trading the day if I lose 3 trades in a row

After you have defined your trading plan you should print it and stick it right to your trading station, and of course check it every time before entering a trade.

As you can see our trading plan is providing us quite a few elements that are vital to our success in every trade:

1. It's giving us clear rules on when to trade, avoiding us stress and randomness in our trading
2. It's protecting our capital and not letting our feelings get in the way when deciding position sizing and where to place our stop losses and how to trail them
3. It's filtering many setups that maybe will be valid according to our trading system, but in which maybe the conditions are not 100% in our favor (think of Napoleon attacking the Duke at Waterloo)

4. It's helping us choosing trades that could give us a greater profit and a smaller loss
5. It's protecting our own psychology and giving us a clear rule on when to stop trading if things are not working and it's better to call it a day

As you can see the benefits of using a Trading Plan are enormous and, in my experience using one is the only way I know to protect your capital and achieve success in consistent and long term way.

If you want to win consistently simply trade consistently and the money will flow in.

Please take a moment to do your trading plan according to your own trading style, your personal rules, and try to think on your limitations, what things make your trading go wrong? when and how are you chronically making mistakes? What are the strengths of your system? When and how is your system working at it's best?

Your 6-step blueprint to become a profitable trader.

After reading all the way to here, you already have the knowledge needed to build a profitable Forex trading strategy however, it's important to approach the developing of your own strategy in a disciplined way. If you have all the steps involved in the developing of your strategy correctly outlined, you will understand better the whole process and how to correct or tweak certain elements of it.

1. Write down your goals for trading Forex (i.e., quit my day job making $4,000 a month of income in 1 year, grow my account to 1 Million in 5 years starting with 10k, or whatever your goal is). This step is important and critical to understand your approach to trading and your overall strategy design. Please set motivating but realistic goals, otherwise you risk leveraging too much and blowing your account.

2. Define how much you will have to earn to achieve your goals in a weekly, monthly, and yearly basis; if you are starting with a sum of money and adding every month, or whatever the numbers must be in order for you to reach your goal. Don't try to figure out the size of the trades or the risk yet, this step is only meant to help you know how much money you will need to make to achieve your goals.

3. Define if you will trade on a position, swing, or scalp basis. You need to assess your personal situation and be realistic about the time you can

commit for trading.

4. Once you have your trading style, time frame and specific money objectives in place, try to define scenarios to achieving them, also considering the risk you are taking.

For example: I need to make $300 a month from my $5,000 account swing trading 2 - 3 trades a week. I will aim for $100 in every trade or 100 pips with a risk of 50 pips. That will make my position $10k and risking 1% to make 2% of my account in every trade. If I make 12 trades a month, I can have up to 5 winning trades, 4 losing trades, and 3 break-even trades and still achieve my goal. Here you can confirm with your trading system expectancy and see if your goal is really possible to achieve.

These are only scenarios and they will never play exactly as you are planning them, but they are important for you to understand what you are trying to achieve and how possible it really is. In this phase, you should back test with the charts to see if what you are planning appears possible and make any necessary adjustments to fine tune your strategy in the back testing, never in real money trading, if you need to tweak do it in demo or back testing only.

5. Open a demo account with the same amount of money you are planning to risk in real life, with the broker you are planning to use, and follow your strategy for at least 4 months. If you need more time, make it 6 months, but not much more than that. If your strategy is not working after 6 months it probably won't work. Don't tweak your strategy a lot. Try to keep it consistent to see how it unfolds for your personal needs and trading style. If you have two strategies that seemed to work good in back testing, go ahead and try them both simultaneously, just avoid strategies that demand too much attention because you could get distracted and not make the testing accurate.

6. After this time, if your strategy is proving to be consistent, go ahead, open a real account, and start trading; make a commitment to stop trading and go back to demo if you lose a specific amount of money, I'd say around 30% of your capital, but you'll know better what this number must be because you'll have all the information to understand if your strategy is working or not.

Final thoughts

Although trading is far from an easy way of earning money, the goal can be achieved if you are willing to maintain the discipline and learning to do it. Remember that you are trading for the long run; start small and build from there. After some time, winnings will start to accumulate and your account can become a real wealth generator.

I will outline a strategy to risk the least possible and keep you motivated to win more, the numbers are examples and you can adapt them to your own situation and liking. But I like big round numbers as milestones.

If you have $10,000 to trade, you can start with $2,000, leave the other $8,000 in your savings account, and when, after some months you grow to $3,000 in your trading account, maybe you can enter another $2,000 from your original $8,000 left.

Now you will trade with $5,000, then after another few months when you reach $7,000 maybe you want to top your account with another $3,000 and make it $10,000.

Now you will be trading $10,000, but your risk will be very limited because $3,000 of that came from your own winnings. After you get to $15,000, you might want to enter your money left and trade with $18,000 and enter your full position. From there, even in a very bad scenario, you can lose up to $8,000 and still have your initial capital.

If you keep on winning and get it to $30,000, you might withdraw $5,000 from the Forex account. Then, after taking the remaining $25,000 to $40,000, you might want to withdraw another $5,000 and take all the risk from your account and recoup the initial investment.

From there, every time you reach some milestone you determine, you will withdraw a portion to enjoy your profits and, at the same time, keep growing your account.

If, at some point, your trading stop working and you lose 30% of your capital, you should go back to demo for at least 4 months to see if you can be profitable again before going back to trade real money.

If you trade focused on achieving the best possible performance, you might go rather fast and double your account every 6-8 months without much trouble, without taking your risk to crazy territories. In this situation, you can start to earn real money after some 18 - 24 months, even if you start with a modest sum of money.

I hope that after reading my story and what I've learned after the wild ride it was to lose all my money and then make it back, I'll save you from making the same mistakes I did. And, if you've already did all and/or other mistakes, maybe this book will help you to get back on your feet and become profitable. If you want to contact me, I decided to open a blog together with this book. It's called:

http://forexlife.me

It's a blog to share ideas on how to achieve freedom and the lifestyle we want, using the Forex markets. It has a lot of interesting and useful information about how to become profitable trading and ways to connect with other traders to make your trading experience less lonely. Please take a visit to the blog or write me to paul@forexlife.me.

The blog has now a 2 hour FREE course on how to start your Journey into Forex Trading to achieve profitability. Please visit this link to access the FREE course:

http://forexlife.me

If you liked the book, please leave a review at Amazon. It will help spread the word and help other people find it and trust it to help them. I thank you very, very much to read all the way to the end of the book and sincerely wish you the very best luck and success in your trading and in your life.